I am
DEAF

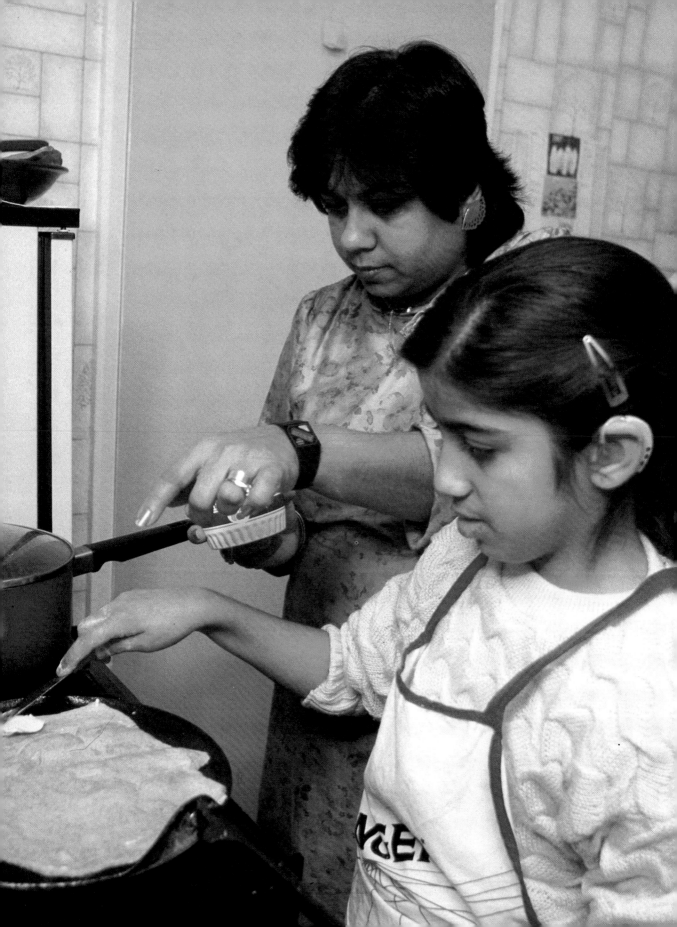

I am
DEAF

Brenda Pettenuzzo
meets
Amina Munir

Photography: Maggie Murray

Consultant:
National Deaf Children's Society

FRANKLIN WATTS

London/New York/Sydney/Toronto

Amina Munir is ten years old. She has been deaf since she was born. She has an older brother, Asim, aged twelve, and two younger brothers, Raza and Mustafa, who are twins, aged eight. Her brothers are also deaf. Her father, Sajjad, is a social worker and her mother, Ghazala, is a Health Education tutor. Amina and her family live on the outskirts of Sheffield.

Contents

The early years	6
At school	12
At home	20
My family	22
Facts about deafness	28
Glossary	31
Index	32

© 1987 Franklin Watts
12a Golden Square
LONDON W1

ISBN: 0 86313 571 4

Series Consultant: Beverley Mathias
Editor: Jenny Wood
Design: Edward Kinsey

Typesetting: Keyspools Ltd

Printed in Great Britain

The Publishers,
Photographer and author
would like to thank Amina
Munir and her family for
their great help and co-
operation in the preparation
of this book.

Brenda Pettenuzzo is a
Science and Religious
Education Teacher at St
Angela's Ursuline Convent
School, a comprehensive
school in the London
Borough of Newham.

The early years

"I have always been deaf. My mum and dad knew, but it was a long time before anyone else would believe them!"

Amina was a "normal" baby. Nothing unusual happened to her when she was born or when she was very small. She did all the things that babies do as they develop into children, but she didn't learn to talk. At first her parents were not too worried. They knew that all babies develop at their own speed. They thought that Amina would be a slow talker, just as she was quicker than some children at other things. But as time went by, they became more and more certain that Amina was not learning to speak because she could not hear properly.

"In the end, I went to see a specialist who knew all about deafness."

When Amina started to attend nursery school, her teachers agreed with her parents. They thought she might be deaf. She was taken to see the doctor but, as she was still very young, it was difficult to test her hearing properly. At last, when she was five-and-a-half years old, a specialist at the hospital confirmed that Amina was deaf, and she was given hearing aids. As soon as she started to wear these aids, Amina began learning to talk! Although Amina was five-and-a-half before she could hear other people speaking, her speech developed quite quickly. None of her friends has any difficulty understanding her.

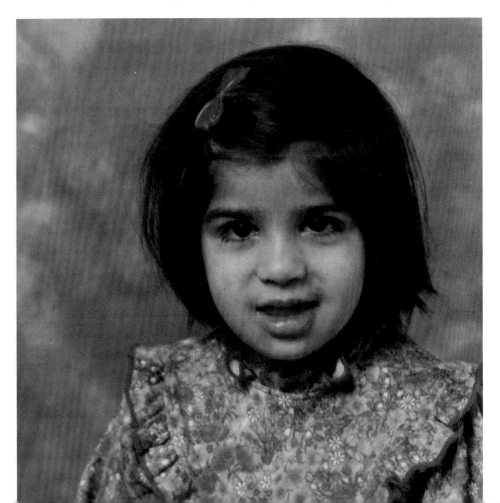

**"My brothers have the same type of deafness as me.
My parents know quite a lot about it now!"**

Asim, Amina's older brother, was found to be deaf
only a short while before Amina. Like her, he always
managed to understand what was going on by lip-
reading. Many deaf children become very skilled at
this, so that adults cannot believe they are deaf at all.
The twins, Mustafa and Raza, did not have to wait so
long. They were four years old when they got their
hearing aids. The whole family is now quite used to
the routine of checking the hearing aids and
attending for check-ups at the hospital.

"My dad is on the committee of the National Deaf Children's Society."

There are several national charities and organisations concerned with deaf people. Many people find that it is very helpful to join a group where everyone has something in common. The parents of deaf children support one another through the National Deaf Children's Society. They also encourage research into deafness, and help to raise money for better aids for deaf children.

"Soon after I wake up each morning I put my hearing aids into my ears."

Amina and her brothers all have the same type of hearing aids for everyday use. These are called "post-aural" aids. This means that they are worn behind the ears. Amina and her brothers wear aids in both ears. Each aid consists of two parts. One part holds the battery and lies behind the ear. The other part, the controls for loudness and tone, is connected to the battery part by a thin tube. This second, control, part fits inside the ear. It is made to fit exactly so that it cannot fall out.

"My hearing aids can't pick out any special sound. They make all the noise round me louder, so I sometimes need a little extra help!"

Amina has a radiophonic aid which helps her to pick out someone's voice when there are other sounds in the room. The person who is speaking has to wear a small microphone and a transmitter. Amina wears a receiver connected to a "loop" which she wears around her neck. This transmits the sound of the person's voice directly to her normal hearing aid. Sometimes her mother wears this microphone at home while Amina is in the garden. Some theatres and cinemas have this type of device built into their sound systems.

At school

"Asim goes to the local comprehensive school now,
but until last year he was at the same school as me."

Amina goes to the local primary school. Her
teachers had help from a specialist teacher at first.
Many have been on courses to help them use the
most effective methods for teaching children whose
hearing is impaired. The specialist teacher still visits
the school every week.

"My teacher is called Mr Shaw. He usually wears the microphone when we are in class."

Amina takes her radiophonic aid to school each day. Mr Shaw wears the microphone while he is teaching Amina's class, and he hands it over to any other teacher who might spend time with them. Mr Shaw already knew about the aid, because he was Asim's class teacher last year. Other teachers soon get used to wearing it when the need arises.

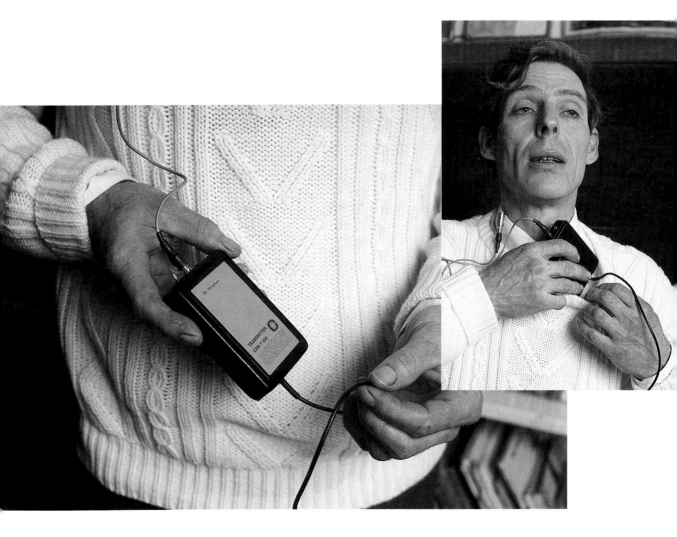

"I sit at the front of the class but we often have to move around the room and work in groups."

Having the radiophonic aid means that Amina can always hear her teacher, wherever she is sitting. Sitting at the front helps her to know whether or not he is speaking directly to her. The microphone makes his voice louder, whether he is speaking to Amina or to someone else. She can hear her friends when they talk to her, through her normal hearing aids. It is easier for her to hear them when they are near. Further-away voices tend to blend together with other sounds and everything gets confusing.

"Each class takes it in turn to do Assembly. The teacher in charge wears a microphone so that my brothers and I can all hear."

The whole school is present at Assembly. Sometimes one class will tell everyone else about some work which they have been doing. The teacher wears a special radiophonic microphone which transmits to Amina's receiver as well as those of her two brothers. This means that all three can hear the teacher, but it doesn't help them to hear the boys and girls who might be reading. Amina tries to watch whoever is speaking so that she can "read" their lips.

"I like most of the things we do at school, especially games and gymnastics."

Being deaf doesn't stop Amina from taking an active part in games. Her hearing aids have to fit well into her ears so that they do not fall out when she is running about. When she is playing a team game such as "Matball" she has to watch the ball carefully. She knows exactly the best person to throw it to, even though she cannot always hear her friend calling out to her.

"I take a packed lunch to school. I usually sit with my best friend and eat it."

Amina has lots of friends, and she likes to chat with them like most boys and girls. It is hard to believe that she hadn't actually heard any words before she was five-and-a-half years old! She has no difficulty in understanding her friends when they talk to her, and they have no difficulty understanding her.

"Although I have check-ups at the hospital, the school nurse checks my eyes and ears just like everyone else."

The school nurse visits Amina's school regularly to do eyesight and hearing tests on all the pupils. The local hospital keeps records of the hearing loss suffered by Amina and her brothers. If the school hearing test showed that anything had changed, the nurse would inform the hospital. Amina and her brothers are all classified as being moderately to severely deaf.

"I have learned to play the recorder at school. We sometimes play at Assembly and at the school concert."

Although Amina is severely deaf, she is not totally deaf. Her hearing aids make the sounds she can hear louder, but not always clearer. Her hearing loss does not stop her from enjoying music, and she particularly enjoys making music. The recorder group meets to practise once a week. Amina also plays at home, and she has taken part in many musical activities at school. Many people whose hearing is impaired share Amina's love of music.

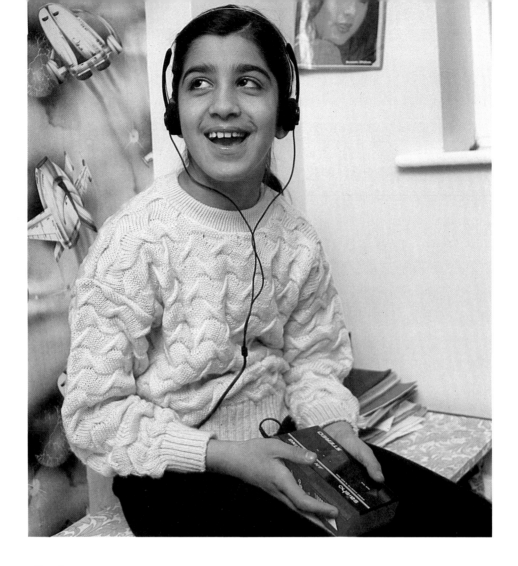

At home

"I have a personal stereo at home, and I love to listen to my music tapes on it."

Her personal stereo is a very convenient way for Amina to listen to music. The headphones mean that the sounds are produced close to her hearing aids, and other sounds are shut out. She enjoys the Indian films which are sometimes shown on television, and has many tapes of the music from these films.

"A lot of the girls who live nearby belong to the Brownies like me."

Amina joined the Brownies when she was seven years old. At first she was very shy and quiet. Her parents were worried that she would not settle down and would not want to go any more. They had a discussion with the Brownie leader about Amina's special needs. For a while the leader took special care of Amina, making sure that she had understood instructions and games. Soon, Amina felt at home and didn't need extra attention any more. Now she goes regularly to meetings, and has been away at weekend camp several times.

My family

"I have lots of aunts, uncles and cousins. Most of them speak English and Urdu, one of the languages of Pakistan. My mum is teaching me Urdu."

Both of Amina's parents have relatives in this country and in Pakistan. They enjoy visiting their families and friends very much, and Amina has travelled widely in this country and to Pakistan. Being deaf presents no problem to her as far as reading and understanding Urdu is concerned. But she has to concentrate very hard when people are speaking to her. Lip-reading in another language is not so easy!

"My dad often talks to us about the traditions of our religion, Islam."

At home there are many reminders of the fact that Amina and her family are of the Muslim faith. Many of the writings of that faith are available in English, which Amina and her brothers can read and understand. The traditional writings are in Arabic script, which Amina and her brothers are learning to understand.

"We all watch television at home, but I sometimes argue with my brothers over which programme we are going to watch."

Each child in the Munir family has a different favourite programme, but sometimes they do agree about what they are going to watch. Amina prefers programmes which have Teletext subtitles. Lots of popular programmes have this feature now and it makes things much easier for deaf people. When they are watching television or listening to the record-player, Amina and her brothers always have the volume too loud for their parents' comfort.

"I like lots of toys and games. At home I play with Lego building bricks."

When she is not playing at her friends' houses, Amina does lots of things at home. She enjoys reading and colouring. Like her brothers, she is also keen on building things with their collection of Lego bricks. When Amina and the twins are busy building, things are very quiet in the house. Each one is concentrating on their own structure and no one speaks!

"I help my mum and dad at home. I love to be in the kitchen when mum is preparing the dinner."

Before the children were found to be deaf, Amina's parents had a lot of difficulty doing ordinary things such as shopping and cooking. It was very dangerous in the kitchen when the children could not see their mum's or their dad's face. At the supermarket all four children had to be close enough to see their parents and be seen. Now that all four children have hearing aids, things are easier. Amina likes to help her dad with the weekly shopping, and she has become quite expert in the kitchen.

"Many of my older relations wear traditional dress all the time, especially those in Pakistan. I have some lovely clothes from there which I save for special occasions."

Amina loves to dress up in her formal clothes for a special family occasion. She keeps photographs to remind her of visits and holidays. Amina and her brothers are the only members of the family to have their type of deafness.

Facts about deafness

There are two main categories of deafness or hearing impairment; to understand the difference between them and their effects it is first necessary to understand the mechanism of hearing.

Sound consists of air movements which are produced whenever an object vibrates. When we perceive or 'hear' a sound it is because the brain has received a nerve impulse which the ear has translated from the vibrations of the air. These vibrations pass along the ear canal and cause the ear-drum to vibrate. This movement is passed on through the middle ear via three tiny bones called the ossicles and finally to the inner ear. Here the Cochlea, which contains very sensitive nerve fibres, converts the vibrations to nervous impulses which are relayed to the brain along the Auditory Nerve. So there are two stages in hearing, the first stage is a physical transmission of the air movements, the second stage is the nervous transmission of the sound to the brain.

If there is a problem in the outer or middle parts of the ear (the Conductive Pathway) then Conductive Deafness will result. In many cases the problem can be treated, or it results in a partial or intermittent loss of hearing. Many children suffer from conductive deafness as a result of infections in the middle ear, or blockages of the Eustachian tubes, which cause the middle ear space to fill up with fluid and prevent the ossicles from vibrating. Both of these conditions can be treated medically or surgically. It is also possible to have malformations of the outer or middle ear which impair the passage of vibratons through the conductive pathway. Deafness may be caused by injury to the ear-drum (for example by a blow to the head) or by a condition called Otosclerosis, in which the ossicles are prevented from vibrating because of overgrowth of bone. Again, in many cases these conditions can be treated.

If there is a problem in the Cochlea, the Auditory Nerve or the hearing centre of the brain, then a different type of deafness will result. This type of deafness is called Sensori-Neural or Nerve Deafness. This type of hearing impairment may vary in degree from mild to total loss of hearing. It is usually not possible to cure nerve deafness, it is considered permanent and is 'treated' by means of hearing aids.

There are many causes of nerve deafness. Some occur before birth, some at or around birth, and some are acquired after birth or later in life. There are several types of inherited nerve deafness, some where the parents themselves (or one of them) are deaf and they pass this trait on to their children, and at least one type where each parent can carry a recessive trait which, when each passes this on to the children, causes deafness. In this case neither parent is deaf but each child conceived has a 1 in 4 chance of having nerve deafness. It is also possible for babies who have no hereditary reasons for being deaf to have their hearing impaired during their time in the womb because of outside influences. This can happen if the mother is infected with a virus such as Rubella (German Measles) and for this reason girls between the ages of 11 and 14 are offered immunisation against this infection through the school health service.

Nerve deafness can occur around the time of birth following shortage of oxygen during a difficult birth, or severe forms of jaundice of the newborn. Many of these problems are becoming increasingly rare as medical techniques for care of 'at risk' babies become more sophisticated.

Children can acquire nerve deafness as a result of certain infections such as meningitis, mumps and measles or the administration of certain drugs.

Most cases of childhood deafness are diagnosed at an early age through parents alerting their G.P.s or through Local Authority clinics and Health Visitors. Babies are given regular developmental checks which include appropriate hearing checks. Once a diagnosis has been made the correct 'remedy' can be given. This might be referral to a specialist for surgery or hearing aids, and also referral to a teacher of the deaf. The earlier a child is helped to hear, the less affected will be that child's speech. Many children benefit from learning to use their residual hearing and to lip-read. Many children also learn to communicate using sign language. There are several television programmes which use a mixture of subtitles and sign language to make their information more accessible to hearing impaired people. An interpreter for the deaf is to be seen at many public gatherings and meetings nowadays, 'signing' what is being said. These developments along with the many technological advances since the invention of the microchip are helping to make life a bit less complicated for those people whose hearing is impaired or non-existent.

Local Education Authorities usually have a service for hearing impaired children as part of their provision. This often includes special units, sometimes attached to ordinary schools, where such children attend school. It also provides peripatetic teachers who visit children in ordinary schools to monitor their progress and provide support.

Over the last twenty years or so, the number of children in normal schools and special units has steadily increased, along with the number of peripatetic teachers. At the same time, the number of children in schools for the deaf has decreased. There might always be children who are so profoundly deaf that only a special school for deaf children will be of benefit to them, but many children benefit socially and educationally from being with hearing children in mainstream schools. Each child is a 'special' case and must be considered alone. When hearing impaired children are placed in mainstream schools, their teachers need to have instruction and support regarding the hearing aids and other equipment, as well as how best to minimise any disadvantage the pupil might suffer.

There are several voluntary organisations which are concerned with the hearing impaired. Many of these have local groups to which deaf people and parents of deaf children belong. Some of the most well known are:

The National Deaf Children's Society
45 Hereford Road,
London, W2 5AH
TEL: 01-229-9272/4

Royal National Institute for the Deaf
105 Gower Street,
London, WC1
TEL: 01-357-8033

British Deaf Association
38 Victoria Place
Carlisle, CA1 1HU
TEL: 0228–48844

1 outer ear
2 ear canal
3 auditory ossicles
4 semicircular canals
5 cochlea
6 auditory nerve
7 eardrum
8 eustachian tube

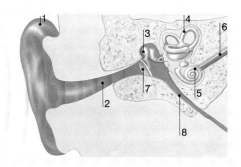

Glossary

Auditory nerve The nerve which is formed when the 30,000 nerve fibres in the Cochlea come together. It carries the nerve impulses from the ear to the brain.

Sign language A system of visual signs made with the hands which can be used for effective communication either to supplement speech or where speech is not possible.

Cochlea The part of the ear which transforms vibration into nerve impulses. In structure it resembles a snail's shell which, unravelled, measures 2.5 cm. Within it are nerve endings embedded in fluid which can create impulses to perceive the pitch and intensity of all audible sounds.

Ear canal The external part of the ear. It extends from the visible ear flap through a bony tunnel to the ear drum. It is lined with cells which produce a protective waxy substance.

Ear drum A thin membrane which vibrates like the skin of a drum as air waves hit it.

Eustachian tubes Canals which connect the middle ear cavity with the back of the throat. This ensures that fluid forming within the ear can drain away, and that the air pressure on the inside of the ear drum is equal to that on the outside. If the tubes become blocked then the middle ear might become infected, or unequal pressure might damage the ear drum.

Lip reading The technique of understanding what is being said by 'reading' the shapes made by the speaker's mouth. This can be quite effective if the speaker is taking care to form the word well, and the 'reader' is experienced enough to guess where there is ambiguity. Many words which sound different look quite similar.

Ossicles The three tiny bones in the middle ear, named (after their shapes) the Hammer, Anvil and Stirrup. They transmit and amplify the vibrations from the ear drum to the cochlea.

Otosclerosis A condition where the ossicles grow larger because of overgrowth of bone, and are no longer able to vibrate.

Peripatetic teacher A specialist teacher who is best used for a short time at each of several schools on a regular basis, rather than all the time at one school.

Index

Assembly 15
Auditory nerve 28, 29, 31

British Deaf Association 30
Brownies 21

Check-up 18
Cochlea 28, 29, 31

Doctor 7

Ear 10, 28, wī
Eustachian tube 28, 31

Family 22
Friends 7, 14, 16, 17, 22, 25

Games 16, 21, 25
German measles 29

Hearing aid 7, 8, 10, 11, 14, 16, 19, 20, 30
Hospital 7, 8, 18

Lip reading 8, 15, 22, 30, 31
Microphone 11, 13, 14, 15

Muslim faith 23

National Deaf Children's Society 9

Pakistan 22
Peripatetic teacher 30, 31
Personal stereo 20
"Post-aural" aids 10

Radiophonic aid 11, 13, 14, 15
Recorder group 19
Research 9
Royal National Institute for the Deaf 30

School 12, 30
School nurse 18
Sign language 30, 31
Specialist 7, 30
Special school 29
Speech 7, 31
Subtitles 24, 30
Supermarket 26
Talking 6, 7
Teacher for the deaf 29
Television 20, 24, 29